2011

To my dear friend Heather.

From June, with very much love.

**Other books in this series:**

HAPPY ANNIVERSARY
To someone special, celebrating your LOVELY NEW BABY
To a very special BROTHER
To a very special DAD
To a very special DAUGHTER
To a very special FRIEND
To a very special GRANDMA
To a very special GRANDPA
To a very special GRANDSON
Wishing you HAPPINESS
To my very special HUSBAND
Someone very special... TO THE ONE I LOVE
To a very special MOTHER
To a very special SISTER
To a very special SON
To a very special TEACHER
Wishing you happiness FOR YOUR WEDDING
To my very special WIFE

Published in 2001 by Helen Exley Giftbooks in Great Britain.
This revised edition published in 2008

12 11 10 9 8 7 6 5 4 3 2

ISBN 13: 978-1-84634-296-7


A copy of the CIP data is available from the British Library on request.

Printed in China.


Helen Exley Giftbooks, 16 Chalk Hill, Watford, Herts WD19 4BG, UK.
www.helenexleygiftbooks.com

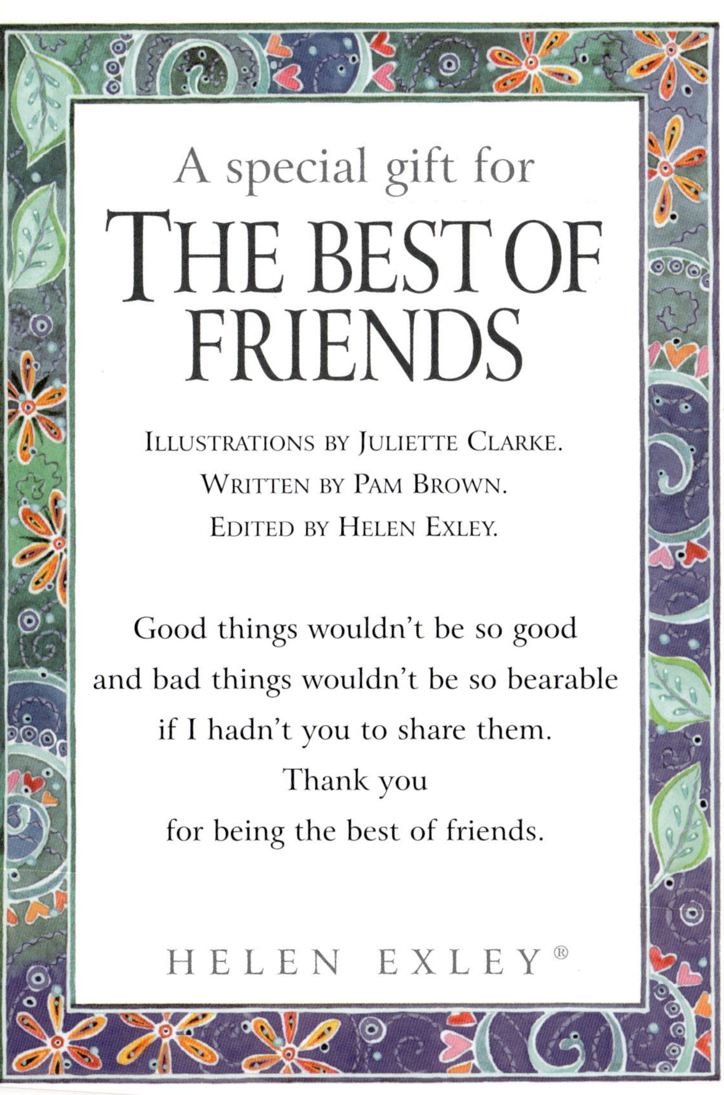

A special gift for

# THE BEST OF FRIENDS

ILLUSTRATIONS BY JULIETTE CLARKE.
WRITTEN BY PAM BROWN.
EDITED BY HELEN EXLEY.

Good things wouldn't be so good
and bad things wouldn't be so bearable
if I hadn't you to share them.
Thank you
for being the best of friends.

HELEN EXLEY®

GIRL FUN!

What's a pop concert without a girl friend
yelling beside you?

A night out with the girls –
a marauding army that no father, no boy, no man,
no world leader can stand against.

There is such a difference between being
a little daft all on your own
– and being a little daft together.

Girls together don't need a reason to giggle themselves into near hysteria. Anything will do.

Basic exchange between girl friends:
"Go on. I dare you."
"Oh, don't be crazy. We can't."
"Of course we can."
"You wouldn't."
"Yes, I would."
"Then do it."
"If you do it."

Women doing the most vital jobs – scientists, nurses, politicians and the like – need short bursts of silliness with girl friends.

## TIME TOGETHER

The whole world over, women and girls
escape the monotonies, the drudgeries,
of everyday existence
– along well-trodden tracks, laughing together
at the river's edge or in the market square,
exchanging ribaldries from balconies, resting
for a moment from the blinding sun or
driving rain. A net of companionship encircling
the planet. Strength regained.
Sympathies exchanged.
Bitterness turned to warmth.
Life made endurable in shared experience,
in laughter and in courage.

Most of all, I thank you for being who you are.
Constant and kind.
Patient and forgiving.
Sharing my journey – the best of all companions.

## GIRL TALK

The thing girl friends do most
and best is talk.

Girl conversations are different to any others.
At each end of the line they curl into
the most comfortable position and
put their feet up –
they intend to be there for a considerable
length of time.

Old friends love to go shopping together,
or to a gallery or concert,
but the part of the outing they love best
is the café with the good coffee
and wonderful cakes where they can
kick off their shoes. And talk.

What's the fun of an adventure if you can't
share it with a friend?

Girl talk is much the same in every age, though differing in detail. Appearance, men, ambitions and despondencies, parents and the future. Boasting of conquests. Dramatizing the dull. Speculating on the half unknown. And since the beginning, bursts of giggling – helpless laughter at the lunacies of life. The happy silliness that keeps the dark at bay.

## UNDERSTANDING ME

You seem to know my needs and answer them
long before I've put them into words.

Who doesn't think it's ridiculous
when you cry in the sad bits at the movies,
and fall off your seat in the silly bits?
Only a friend.

Every good thing is better if you can share it
with a friend.

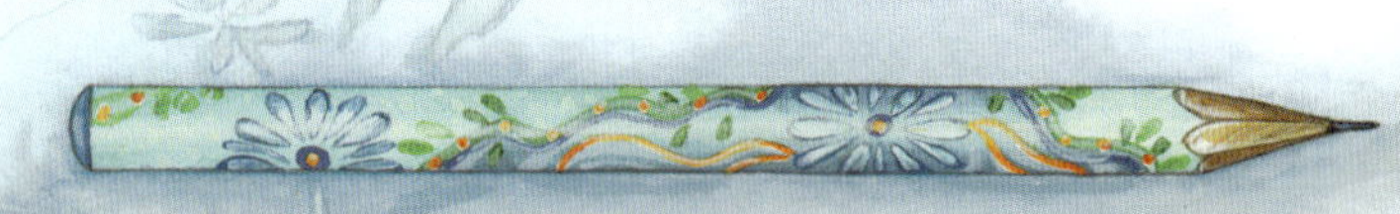

We don't need to ask each other.
We know whether we take tea black or white,
whether we eat spinach, whether we need
extra pillows. We know the sort
of play the other likes, which books, what music.
We know each other's most-loved flower and scent.
We know each other's oddities.
And so each meeting is like coming home.

Thank you for sitting very still and nodding
in all the right places when I told you some tale
of injustice and wrong doing and worked myself
to fever pitch.
And making me a cup of tea when I had done.

Sharer of anxieties.
Sharer of silly jokes.
Sharer of excitements.
Thank you for everything.

# MY TRUSTED SUPPORTER

Friends are there when your hopes
are frayed and your nerves are knotted.
Talking about nothing in particular,
you can feel the tangles untwist.

There are days in a girl's life
when she needs a friend,
chocolate and a box of tissues.

A friend gives you more than
your fair share of her umbrella.

Ask a friend to your party.
Lose track of her.
Find her in the kitchen washing the dishes.

Friendship can make the unbearable bearable.

A friend like you is an old
and well worn dressing-gown
to wrap around me when
the world seems dark and cold.

Friends make it possible to live in a cruel world.

Hand on heart, I can say to you, “Thank you. I don’t know how I would have managed without you.”

SHOPPING SPREE!

The clarion call to almost all girl friends like us is "Sale!" "Special Offer!"

Haven't we had fun getting into things – and out of them?

We girl friends hunt the sales in packs,
pouncing, worrying and dragging off our prey –
to discover later what we've actually caught.

With you I can have an afternoon of luxury –
padding around the carpeted expanse
of splendid stores, fingering cloth,
admiring dinner services and fragile glasses,
sniffing scent, trying hats.
With you I come home
with a paperback and a hair brush.
Exhausted. Happy. Solvent.

You are the one, the only, person with whom
I'll shop for clothes.
Because you're the only one who will say
"Have you seen yourself from behind?!"

SHE PROTECTS YOU – FROM YOURSELF!

A friend tells you when the label is sticking
out of your sweater,
when you have it on inside out,
when you've a gaping hole in your stockings,
when you've sauce on your chin,
when you've only made up one eye.
And when your skirt is caught in your underwear.

A good friend knows when to praise
your appearance and when to shout with horror...
And so save you from cowering embarrassment.

Friends egg you on. Best friends hold you back.

Mothers and fathers can't prevent a girl from
acquiring an enormous tattoo of an enveloping
boa constrictor. Only a girl friend can persuade her
a very small rosebud is a better idea.

Every girl, every woman is under pressure
from her peers and colleagues to do things
to keep in with the crowd. Only a very good friend
can talk through the possible consequences and
not be condemned as a killjoy.

A good friend gives you the courage to be a coward.

Thank you for showing me that being made to look
ridiculous isn't the end of the world.

## TO MY RESCUE – AGAIN

You have a way of being there when
I most need you.
In great emergencies. In moments of celebration...
And when the washing machine floods or
the casserole burns quietly to a cinder.

A friend is the person to whom
you'll open the door when it's a bad hair day,
when you have chickenpox,
when you've just flooded the kitchen,
when the cat's used his box enthusiastically
– when nobody else will do.

Friends are very good at emergencies.
They've had a lot of practice.

The sad thing about human beings
is that they never believe that bad things
can happen to them – only to other people.
It is our friends who help us through
our disillusions.

Friends know you better than you know yourself
– and unobtrusively stand by
to pick up the pieces.

## SMALL, CRAZY SURPRISES

A girl friend knows what you want and need.
A pot of zinnias. A Battenberg cake.
A new detective story. Pesto. Compost.
Licorice. Jane Austen.
Things that no one else would think of
in a hundred years.

Friends carry a list in their heads:
clothes sizes, best-loved scents,
preferred shades, best-loved flowers
and edible delights.
Friends find you Little Treats.

Other people's presents are useful, sensible
or totally expected.
Yours come in strange-shaped packages
and wheeze or click or rattle –
or lie there defying all guessing.

Friends give you Unbirthday presents.

Thank you for the small, crazy surprises
that light up the dull days and the sad days
and the days that lie like cold porridge
on the stomach.

With you, I can always say, with all my heart,
"Oh! I've always wanted one of those!"

## MISSING YOU ROTTEN

We live so far apart, and yet, somehow,
we have kept track of one another.
Too long a silence and each begins
to worry. We need to know the other is there –
sharing the planet, safe and sound, under
the self-same star. The link we fashioned so long
ago is thin as a thread but strong as steel.

You are always there, unwavering in kindness and
concern – certainty in an uncertain world.

Girl friends have bigger telephone bills
than Hollywood tycoons.

Thank you for phoning me for ridiculous reasons.

The day started badly.
It was raining.
The milk was sour.
My email was dead. A fistful of bills.
A drift of circulars.
Gloom. Doom.
But then you rang.
And made me laugh.

A little pleasure – putting a red ring
round a calendar date to show
I'll see you soon.

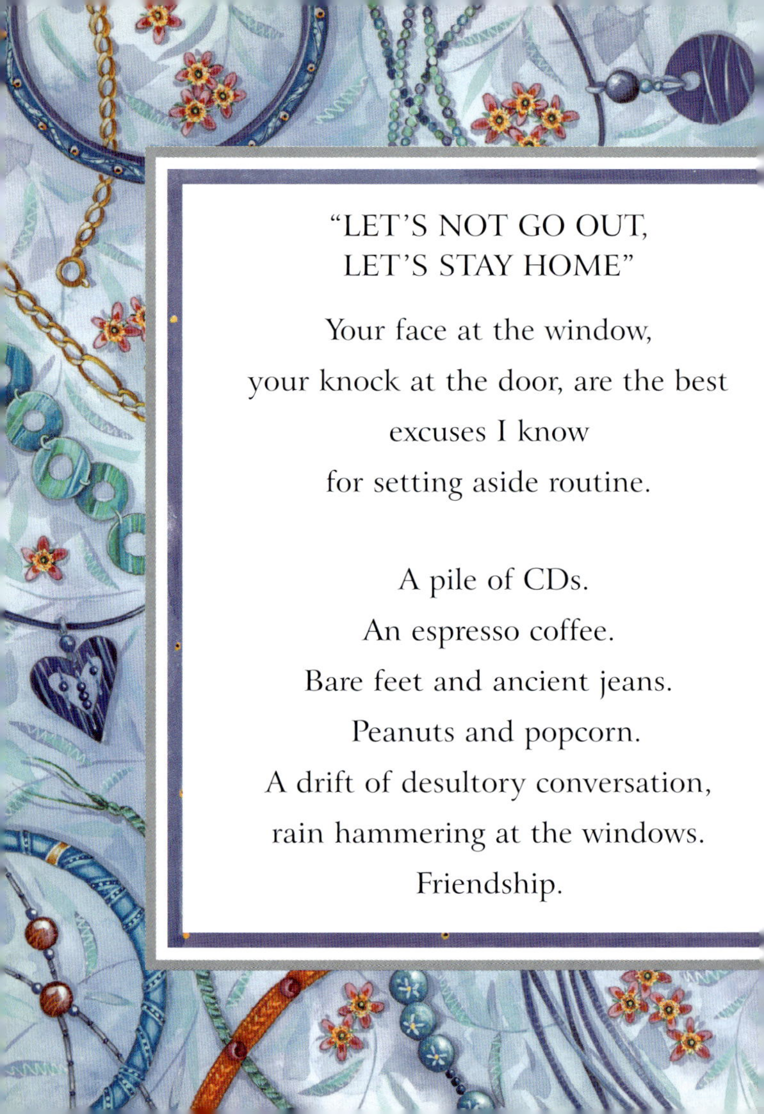

## "LET'S NOT GO OUT, LET'S STAY HOME"

Your face at the window,
your knock at the door, are the best
excuses I know
for setting aside routine.

A pile of CDs.
An espresso coffee.
Bare feet and ancient jeans.
Peanuts and popcorn.
A drift of desultory conversation,
rain hammering at the windows.
Friendship.

A discussion between
friends about which cinema
to go to, invariably ends up
with them staying home, watching
a DVD of Pride and Prejudice,
and making a major decision
on a change of career.

Thank heaven we girls have girl
friends with whom we can gloom,
discuss the impossibility of all men
and eat huge quantities
of chocolate ice-cream.

## ALWAYS THERE, ALWAYS LOYAL

Friends who have gone
through hard times together, have a bond
outsiders can never understand.

You have always been there when I needed you
– to hold my hand or pat my back
or wipe away my tears, or share my laughter.
May I always be there for you.

Friendship is what shows us that we
are not alone in any joy or any sorrow.

Thanks for backing me when you were
absolutely sure that I wasn't wrong.
And being understanding when I was.

When I feel myself a failure,
inadequate, stupid, a
nothing creature – you do not
turn away, exasperated by my gloom,
but lure me back to life.

When exam results are nothing
like I'd hoped, who do I turn to?
I give a watery grin –
and rejoin the human race.

How fortunate I am to have
a friend like you. I look back
on the happy times we've known –
and wish you a year, a future,
packed with delights.